BRITISH
WARSHIPS
& AUXILIARIES

A Sea Harrier launches from HMS ILLUSTRIOUS;
SOUTHAMPTON and CORNWALL in the background.

D0316982

THE ROYAL NAVY

The sea covers 70.8% of the world's surface and two thirds of the world's population live within 100 miles of the coast. Over 150 of the 185 member states of the UN are coastal states. Britain has a world-wide expatriate community of over 10 million and UK citizens make 34 million journeys abroad each year. The UK is the world's 6th largest trading nation exporting a higher % of GDP than France, Germany, USA and Japan. We export more than a quarter of everything we produce of which almost 95% by weight (Some £250 billion of our trade) is transported by sea. This includes oil, food and the raw materials needed by industry. We invest a higher % of our GDP abroad than any other country. The UK Marine sector value (not including fishing) is £25bn per annum, 6% of a rising world total and some 5% of UK GDP. Offshore oil and gas contributes approximately £4Bn to the UK balance of payments. The UK attracts over 40% of Japanese and US investments in the EU.

The latest statistics from the Government report that the UK merchant shipping sector is still increasing. The Fleet is the 13th largest in the world and second in the EU after Greece. UK owners possess 594 ships of which 366 are registered in the UK. A further 171 trading vessels are registered in the Isle of Man and Channel Islands. There are approximately 27,000 British merchant seafarers.

The UK has 10,500 miles of coastline and in an average year RN aircraft expect to conduct over 500 search and rescue operations.The UK has an Economic Fishing Zone of 270,383 square miles (3 times the land area of the UK). Under the DEFRA contract, the Fishery Protection Squadron (FPS) was required to conduct 950 patrol days in 02/03. Waters north of 56 degrees north are the responsibility of the Scottish Fisheries Protection Agency. The remaining 140,000 square miles of ocean encompass some of the richest fishing grounds in the world. 60% of all fish landed in the EU comes from UK waters.

(Figures supplied by MoD)

Against such a background the need for a modern, flexible and strong Royal Navy to preserve our interests, protect our seafarers, maintain our trade routes and police our fishing grounds, would seem to be common sense. In the wake of the 11 September attrocities in the United States a commitment to take the fight to the terrorists must also be included. And yet as these tasks place ever increasing demands on an already stretched Fleet, the RN, already cut to the bone, continues to see ships axed from the frontline fleet. Although the RN will steadfastly try to meet all of the demands placed upon it with its usual can do attitude, there will be a time, in the not too distant future, when it will have to put up its hands and say "Stop!"

Over the following pages, as we look at the current operations of the RN, the state of the Fleet, and what the future holds, it is hard to be optimistic, but there is light at the end of the tunnel - were I a doctor I might diagnose the patient at present as critical, but given the correct treatment, the prognosis could be fine, but the next few years are going to be decisive.

Current Operations

As we close for press the RN has ships deployed to all four corners of the World, engaged in numerous operations. Whilst most of the Rns good work is done out of the public gaze, the media places it under minute scrutiny whenever anything goes wrong.

The year 2002 started at a very high tempo of activity as Exercise Saif Sareea 2001 had transitioned into Operation Veritas. Almost overnight many of the Rns operational assets in the Middle East were diverted from an exercise situation into a high profile war against terrorism. The fact that ships were easily able to slip into a new role on completion of the exercise was an excellent example of the value of seapower - and flexibility. The role of the RN in the current war against terrorism raises many concerns about their susceptability to attack from small craft. The attack on the USS COLE in Aden followed by the attack on the French supertanker LIMBURG in the same area must raise many questions for world leaders. Will these fanatics be driving their small plastic boats filled with explosives into a cruise liner for their next headline grabbing attack? Understandably the British Seamen in the NUMAST union had their leaders calling on Foreign Office and MoD officials asking for more protection but at the time of writing there were no obvious signs of any assets being provided.

Throughout the year the ships of the Atlantic Patrol Ship (North) have been enjoying tremendous success in the war against drugs in the Caribbean. As I write this it has been reported that GRAFTON has made the third seizure during her current deployment, removing drugs from the dealers with an estimated street value of £3 million. Her previous seizure saw the interception of £75 million worth of cocaine. She is not alone - earlier in the year NEWCASTLE enjoyed similar success, as have COVENTRY, NORTHUMBERLAND, MARLBOROUGH and BRAVE in previous years. Next time the RN agree to a TV fly on the wall documentary, perhaps they should document the Counter-Drugs operations, rather than months of endless interdiction operations in the Adriatic. This operation is well suited to the RN though it is perhaps time that consideration was given to procurement of vessels more suited to this type of surveillance and intercept mission. The requirement for expensive and sophisticated ASW and Harpoon equipped frigates to conduct these tasks must be questionable.

The unfortunate grounding of the destroyer NOTTINGHAM off the Australian Coast, whilst deployed to the Far East, hit newspaper headlines around the world. Without exception the reports centred on the embarrassment to the RN of having their warship aground. Much speculation ensued as to who was responsible, who should carry the can and should the ship be scrapped. Negative press and mocking headlines around the world. There was a memorable scene in the Hollywood blockbuster *Apollo 13*. As Mission Control prepared to get the crippled spacecraft to earth, the PR guru whispered that this was going to be NASAs worst disaster. The Head of the mission turned on him saying that "This would be their finest hour". The moments immediately after the NOTTINGHAM grounding were, for the young men and women onboard the destroyer, without doubt - , "their finest hour". Perhaps it wasn t evident until the vessel was lifted clear of the water - but that crew put into action years of damage control training and fought relentlessly to save their ship. One look at the damage to the hull revealed just how close she had come to sinking. With major compartments breached, water coming in through massive rents in the hull, no power, no communications and no lighting, the crew won the battle to stem the flow of water and over the ensuing days secured their ship. It is a tragedy that the press chose to seek ridicule and place blame. It is to be hoped that when the dust settles proper credit is paid to that crew who, as one, upheld the proudest traditions of the Service.

3

While other destroyers and frigates continue their cycle of deployments in support of the Falkland Islands, NATO squadrons in the Atlantic and Mediterranean, Armilla patrol in the Gulf and anti-terror operations in the Indian Ocean, Arabian Sea and Red Sea, the smaller ships of the MCM squadrons and the patrol vessels continue operating on the frontline.

Royal Navy Minecountermeasures Vessels have been operating in the Baltic, assisting the former Soviet Baltic States to clear their harbours and sealanes of hundreds of tons of live ordnance, a job carried out with extreme professionalism and again out of sight of the public (another TV opportunity?). As we go to press four MCMVs are heading for Saudi Arabia for exercises in the Persian Gulf. The patrol vessels have not been neglected either - LEEDS CASTLE continues to operate in the inhospitable waters of the South Atlantic and the converted Hunt class maintain their vigil around the waters of Northern Ireland. Although this operation is being scaled down - it remains an important task. The reduction in the RN deployments to the Province has resulted in the release of two Patrol Vessels to Gibraltar, where, the Gibraltar Patrol Squadron and its two P2000s have been maintaining anti-terror and port security patrols for many years. The recent terrorist threats to Naval Shipping in the Mediterranean and in particular the Straits of Gibraltar, have resulted in the more capable GREYFOX and GREYWOLF being redeployed for trials to test their suitability for such open water operations.

The State of the Fleet

Submarines

The Vanguard class continue on their cycle of deterrent patrols with one submarine normally on patrol. The Vanguard refit facilities have been completed at Devonport and the first boat, VANGUARD arrived in February to begin her two year refit.

The hunter killer force was heavily tarnished by the reactor faults which resulted in supension of operations in 2000. In 2001 things were better with three submarines being involved in the opening attacks of the war against terror. However, recent events are bringing the service back into the public eye once again (it can only be bad news). In November TRAFALGAR, whilst operating on both JMC and Submarine Commanding Officers Qualifying Course, hit the seabed off the Isle of Skye. The vessel is due to be out of service for several months whilst surveys, safety checks and repairs are conducted. Within weeks it was revealed that two submarines, SCEPTRE and SOVEREIGN have lain idle at Rosyth and Faslane respectively for over two years, in the case of SCEPTRE, not having been on patrol since the end of her refit in the summer of 2000!

The future for the SSNs looks bleak with the recent announcement that the new Astute class are running a further 18 months behind schedule. This means that unless one of the older S class is run on beyond its announced decommissioning date, the submarine force is going to have to run a reduced number of boats for several years.

Carriers

It has been a mixed year for the aircraft carriers. The refit cycle has meant that at the end of the year there was only one carrier, ARK ROYAL, available for operations. ILLUSTRIOUS entered refit at Rosyth in October 2002 and INVINCIBLE will not be ready to rejoin the fleet until Spring 2003. ARK ROYAL deployed to the Mediterranean as part of Argonaut 2002 - with the Merlin helicopter embarked. She returned to port in November.

On the bright side the Government has reaffirmed its commitment to the future carrier programme by selecting the Joint Strike Fighter as its next carrier borne aircraft. The excitement following the announcement must be tempered by the fact that the selected aircraft is the STOVL version, and that the two carriers are to be built with ski-jumps rather than catapults and arrestor wires. It is hard to see the thinking behind this selection process. These huge vessels, big enough to operate any current fixed wing naval fighter, will be restricted to STOVL operations. Further, the lack of arrestor gear and catapults has once again committed the Fleet Air Arm to operating helicopter borne AEW aircraft and the supersonic JSF will be handicapped in both range and payload by the limitations imposed by vertical flight. The announcements that both teams competing for the carrier build programme prefer Rosyth as their final assembly yard is good news as nuclear submarine refit work at the Scottish base comes to an end.

Amphibious Vessels

Without doubt the flavour of the moment is Amphibiosity . For many years it has been neglected, but at last modernisation is on the horizon. The ageing LPD FEARLESS returned to Portsmouth for the last time in March 2002, leaving OCEAN as the RNs only available amphibious asset. Herself overworked she has spent the latter half of 2002 in drydock whilst modifications and repairs are undertaken. Delayed yet again ALBION is not nowscheduled to enter service until July 2003, which would put her availability for operations around six months later. She is scheduled to be joined by her sistership BULWARK at the year s end - but until then, there will be no LPD capability available.
The elderly LSLs of the Sir class are also to be replaced. The four ships of the Bay class are so much larger and more capable than their predecessors that they will be redesignated in service as LSD(A). To round up the modernisation of the amphibious forces all six Strategic Sealift RoRo vessels should be in service by the end of 2003, bringing a much needed increase in sealift capability for the Joint Rapid Reaction Force.

Escorts

It is here that the most concern must rest. Already painfully overstretched and operating some tonnage well past its prime, the destroyer and frigate force continues to suffer from salami slicing cuts. Following rumours in the press of more large scale cuts to the escort force, to fund the future carriers (the loss of six escorts under SDR were sold as payment for the carrier programme; further cuts could see the RN paying twice) SHEFFIELD was paid off early. The reasoning behind this reduction below the SDR agreed minimum of 32 escorts, was accredited to new refit cycles. By extending the period between Type 23 refits from 9 to 10 years it was assessed that the RN could lose a frigate and still field the 26 operational vessels as stipulated under SDR. The quite unbelievable aspect of this is that it was done at the same time as NOTTINGHAM was severely damaged on the other side of the world and obviously out of action for a very long time. How can the Government reconcile paying off a frigate whilst at the same time knowing that a destroyer is going to be out of action for many months, possibly years, outside of the normal refit cycle. A further argument for paying off SHEFFIELD was the saving of £20 million operating costs (this shortly after a spending increase of £3.5 billion!) To date it has cost almost £20 million to bring NOTTINGHAM back to the UK to be surveyed! There is no slack in the escort force - no reserve ships to call on should a ship be unexpectedly put out of operation (To pile misery upon misery a cross Channel Ferry hit ST. ALBANS, causing considerable damage to the superstructure. A brand new frigate, she has now been withdrawn from operations, well outside of her scheduled refit cycle). With no new escort tonnage being available until 2007 the RN cannot afford to lose another escort. Persistent reports in the press of massive cuts and interest in Type 22 and Type 23 frigates from foreign navies does nothing to dispel that feeling that the Treasury are trying to sell off the family silver.

Minor Vessels

The RN MCM forces are widely regarded as amongst the best in the world, though in recent years they too have seen their numbers reduced. Two Hunt class have been sold to Greece and a Single Role Minehunter has been reduced to a static training role. Whilst it could be argued that there is not really a credible mine threat at present, it doesn't take much imagination to see the chaos that could be wrought by a terror organisation wishing to inflict serious disruption to the country. A couple of years ago Britain was almost brought to its knees by a few motivated people picketing fuel depots ashore. Imagine the consequences if a terrorist organisation placed, or even intimated that they had placed, mines around a handful of our most strategically important ports. In this light it is amazing to see a relatively new ship - CROMER - paid off from the small MCM Fleet and relegated to an alongside role as a floating classroom at Dartmouth during the year and seemingly a sister ship - BRIDPORT - heading for a similar fate.

At the start of the New Year the first of three new fishery protection vessels should be in service. Eventually three vessels (owned by Vosper Thornycroft and leased to the MoD) will have replaced the original seven "deep sea" vessels of the FPS. Although advertised as being more capable than the vessels that they replace, three vessels cannot be in seven places at one time! These vessels are also to be operated on a five year public finance initiative. The whole subject of Fishery Protection is one of a once important task being rapidly downsized (and eventually quietly forgotten?) as the country is forced into a new future within Europe. After five years, no doubt we will see these vessels operating with a new role and "our" fish available for anyone to plunder.

New tonnage has started to arrive to give the Survey Squadron a reprieve from its highly rundown state. A wartime role for these vessels seems to have given the whole of the Hydrographic Branch a reprieve from possible extinction and is much welcomed.

Sea Harrier

Undoubtedly the decision to pay-off the Sea Harrier in 2004 was the biggest body blow the RN had to take during the year. Inevitably their demise will put ships in unnecessary danger if an expeditionary force is to be deployed any distance away from shores - where friendly shore based fighter cover is available. It is a decision that should be hotly contested and reversed before time, and personnel, run out. Despite its shortcomings in extremely hot climates, the capability of the Sea Harrier has been praised extensively by senior officers and it seems this obviously Treasury inspired cut is indeed a cut too far and should be fought vigorously if any meaningful RN task group is to be deployable worldwide. Even though the demise of the Sea Harrier and the advent of its replacement may only be a relative few years away, the loss of junior Sea Harrier pilots will be one extemely difficult to remedy when the JSF starts to become available. The loss of experienced fixed wing pilots and the training of their replacements is a major cause for concern. The establishment of 727 NAS to offer free flying lessons, at Plymouth Airport, to potential recruits, is a step in the right direction.

Primary Casualty Receiving Ships

An answer to a question in the House of Commons in the Autumn of 2002 revealed that the Primary Casualty Receiving Ship project was not proceeding to plan and the building of the two promised ships was being put back until "the end of the decade". The goalposts appear to be moving (the size and capability has been downgraded) and the whole project has taken a lower priority as the year ticked by. Coupled with the problems throughout the Defence Medical Services where cuts made a few years ago have been acknowledged as being too severe SDR intentions are not coming to fruition. There is doubtless a requirement for a whole new hospital to be resurrected for totally tri-service use. Many of the staff allocated to NHS hospitals in Portsmouth and Plymouth under the current system as being redeployable - frequently at short notice - create a major problem for the NHS. Surely there is scope for one of these hospitals to be built within the hull of something of supertanker size that can spend 95% of its time alongside, but is readily and easily deployable should an appropriate situation arise.

Manpower

As we closed for press a national firemen's strike was taking place and over 3,000 members of the RN were brought ashore, ships programmes having to be altered to do so, and units withdrawn from exercises, as all three services prepared for the national emergency. One of the major problems was that, compared to the strike of 1977, there is no longer a ready reserve of manpower to draw on for these national emergencies. Most RN shore billets, which formed that ready pool have been taken over by civilians.

Opportunities to show the Navy off have not been fully grasped. The Golden Jubilee was a lost opportunity, the Armed Forces spectacular happening well after the main weekend of celebrations and receiving little publicity - and my only abiding memory of Plymouth Navy Days - being surveyed for my views whilst there and being solicited to buy time share days later by a company using that information!

The Future

When looking through the Government supplied "rose coloured glasses" the RN is looking in good shape. There is a vast re-equipment programme underway. Amphibious forces are at last due to get much improved vessels and increased sealift; the Fleet Air Arm are to get supersonic fixed wing aircraft to operate from two new super carriers; new large state of the art air defence destroyers have been ordered and a new class of nuclear powered submarines is under construction. But let's not lose sight of the fact that this capability will not be fully available for perhaps 5-10 years. In the meantime, the Navy must soldier on with old and out of date tonnage; in some areas capability will continue to be withdrawn before new equipment arrives to replace it. The Navy has lost a lot of good ships to pay for this new future. Whilst it struggles on to bridge the gap between old and worn out ships, and promised new capability, rumours continue of more cuts to come (SHEFFIELD has already been sacrificed).

The RN cannot truly remain a credible force if the Government continues to "salami slice" what remains of the active fleet during these crucial gap years before the promised new tonnage arrives.

SHIPS OF THE ROYAL NAVY
Pennant Numbers

Ship	Pennant Number	Page	Ship	Pennant Number	Page
Aircraft Carriers					
INVINCIBLE	R05	13	MARLBOROUGH	F233	18
ILLUSTRIOUS	R06	13	IRON DUKE	F234	18
ARK ROYAL	R07	13	MONMOUTH	F235	18
			MONTROSE	F236	18
Destroyers			WESTMINSTER	F237	18
			NORTHUMBERLAND	F238	18
NEWCASTLE	D87	16	RICHMOND	F239	18
GLASGOW	D88	16			
EXETER	D89	16	**Submarines**		
SOUTHAMPTON	D90	16			
NOTTINGHAM	D91	16	VANGUARD	S28	10
LIVERPOOL	D92	16	VICTORIOUS	S29	10
MANCHESTER	D95	17	VIGILANT	S30	10
GLOUCESTER	D96	17	VENGEANCE	S31	10
EDINBURGH	D97	17	TRENCHANT	S91	11
YORK	D98	17	TALENT	S92	11
CARDIFF	D108	16	TRIUMPH	S93	11
			SCEPTRE	S104	12
Frigates			SPARTAN	S105	12
			SPLENDID	S106	12
KENT	F78	18	TRAFALGAR	S107	11
PORTLAND	F79	18	SOVEREIGN	S108	12
GRAFTON	F80	18	SUPERB	S109	12
SUTHERLAND	F81	18	TURBULENT	S110	11
SOMERSET	F82	18	TIRELESS	S117	11
ST ALBANS	F83	18	TORBAY	S118	11
CUMBERLAND	F85	20			
CAMPBELTOWN	F86	20	**Assault Ships**		
CHATHAM	F87	20			
CORNWALL	F99	20	OCEAN	L12	14
LANCASTER	F229	18	ALBION	L14	15
NORFOLK	F230	18	BULWARK	L15	15
ARGYLL	F231	18			

HMS Victorious

VANGUARD CLASS

Ship	Pennant Number	Completion Date	Builder
VANGUARD	S28	1992	VSEL
VICTORIOUS	S29	1994	VSEL
VIGILANT	S30	1997	VSEL
VENGEANCE	S31	1999	VSEL

Displacement 15,000 tons (dived) **Dimensions** 150m x 13m x 12m **Speed** 25 + dived
Armament 16 - Trident 2 (D5) missiles, 4 Torpedo Tubes **Complement** 132

Notes
After the first successful UK D5 strategic missile firing in May '94 the first operational
patrol was carried out in early '95 and a patrol has been constantly maintained ever since.
These submarines have two crews each to maintain the maximum period on patrol.
Construction costs of the last, VENGEANCE, are estimated at £863 million. VANGUARD
entered refit at Devonport in February 2002 and is due to complete in 2004.

HMS Triumph

TRAFALGAR CLASS

Ship	Pennant Number	Completion Date	Builder
TRENCHANT	S91	1989	Vickers
TALENT	S92	1990	Vickers
TRIUMPH	S93	1991	Vickers
TRAFALGAR	S107	1983	Vickers
TURBULENT	S110	1984	Vickers
TIRELESS	S117	1985	Vickers
TORBAY	S118	1986	Vickers

Displacement 4,500 tons **Dimensions** 85m x 10m x 8m **Speed** 30 + dived **Armament** 5 Torpedo Tubes **Complement** 110.

Notes

Enhanced development of the Swiftsure Class. Quieter, faster and with greater endurance than their predecessors. Tomahawk Cruise Missiles fitted in TRIUMPH, TRAFALGAR and TURBULENT. It is expected Tomahawk will eventually be fitted in all of these boats. Decommissioning dates have been announced by the MoD as: TRAFALGAR (2007); TURBULENT (2008); TIRELESS (2011); TALENT (2017); TRIUMPH (2019); TORBAY (2021) and TRENCHANT (2023).

● CHRIS ROGERS

HMS Splendid

SWIFTSURE CLASS

Ship	Pennant Number	Completion Date	Builder
SCEPTRE	S104	1978	Vickers
SPARTAN	S105	1979	Vickers
SPLENDID	S106	1980	Vickers
SOVEREIGN	S108	1974	Vickers
SUPERB	S109	1976	Vickers

Displacement 4,500 tons dived **Dimensions** 83m x 10m x 8m **Speed** 30 knots + dived **Armament** 5 Torpedo Tubes **Complement** 116.

Notes
All are based at Faslane. Tomahawk is fitted in SPLENDID and SPARTAN. It is thought that at least one vessel has the capability to deliver special forces. Decommissioning dates have been announced by the MoD as: SPLENDID (2003); SOVEREIGN (2005); SUPERB (2006); SPARTAN (2006) and SCEPTRE (2010).

• MOD/CROWN COPYRIGHT

HMS Ark Royal

INVINCIBLE CLASS

Ship	Pennant Number	Completion Date	Builder
INVINCIBLE	R05	1979	Vickers
ILLUSTRIOUS	R06	1982	Swan Hunter
ARK ROYAL	R07	1985	Swan Hunter

Displacement 20,700 tons **Dimensions** 206m x 32m x 6.5m **Speed** 28 knots **Armament** 2 - 20mm guns, 3 Phalanx/Goalkeeper **Aircraft** 8 - Sea Harrier, 12 - Sea King (6 Merlin on ARK ROYAL) **Complement** 682 + 366 Fleet Air Arm.

Notes
Recent practice has seen only one carrier operational. ARK ROYAL recommissioned in November 2001. INVINCIBLE is scheduled to return to the fleet in 2003 following refit. ILLUSTRIOUS is in refit at Rosyth throughout the year. All can assume the LPH role. Vessels frequently deploy with RAF Harrier GR7s.

13

● MoD/CROWN COPYRIGHT

HMS Ocean

LPH

Ship	Pennant Number	Completion Date	Builder
OCEAN	L12	1998	Kvaerner

Displacement 21,578 tonnes **Dimensions** 208m x 34m x 6.6m **Speed** 17 knots **Armament** 3 x Phalanx, 6 x 30mm BMARC guns **Complement** Ship 284, Squadrons 180, Embarked force 800.

Notes
Can carry 12 Sea King and 6 Lynx or Gazelle helicopters. Frequently employed as the flagship of the UK Amphibious Ready Group. RAF Chinook helicopters are normally carried as an integral part of the ship's air group, but they are unable to be stowed below decks.

HMS Albion

LPD
ALBION CLASS

Ship	Pennant Number	Completion Date	Builder
ALBION	L14	2003	BAE Systems
BULWARK	L15	2003	BAE Systems

Displacement 18,500 tons, 21,500 tons (flooded) **Dimensions** 176m x 25.6m x 6.1m
Speed 18 knots **Armament** 2 x CIWS, 2 x 20mm guns (single) **Complement** 325
Military Lift 303 troops, with an overload capacity of a further 405.

Notes
The first of two LPD(R)s ALBION is scheduled to be delivered in July 2003. Vehicle deck
capacity for up to six Challenger 2 tanks or around 30 armoured all-terrain tracked vehicles. Floodable well dock, with the capacity to take either four utility landing craft (each
capable of carrying a Challenger 2 tank) or shelter a US Landing Craft Air Cushion
(LCAC). Four smaller landing craft on davits, each capable of carrying 35 troops. Two-
spot flight deck able to take medium support helicopters and stow a third. Deck is capable of taking the Chinook. Does not have a hangar but does have equipment needed to
support aircraft operations. Has diesel/electric propulsion. Sistership BULWARK is
expected to be delivered in December 2003. FEARLESS was withdrawn from service in
March 2002. She is likely to be sold for scrap.

• DAVE CULLEN

HMS Southampton

DESTROYERS
SHEFFIELD CLASS
(Type 42) Batch 1 & 2

Ship	Pennant Number	Completion Date	Builder
NEWCASTLE	D87	1978	Swan Hunter
GLASGOW	D88	1978	Swan Hunter
EXETER	D89	1980	Swan Hunter
SOUTHAMPTON	D90	1981	Vosper T.
NOTTINGHAM	D91	1982	Vosper T.
LIVERPOOL	D92	1982	C. Laird
CARDIFF	D108	1979	Vickers

Displacement 3,660 tons **Dimensions** 125m x 15m x 7m **Speed** 29 knots **Armament** 1 - 4.5-inch gun, 4 - 20mm guns, Sea Dart Missile System: 2 - Phalanx, Lynx Helicopter, 6 Torpedo Tubes **Complement** 266.

Notes
BIRMINGHAM which paid off in late 1999 was scrapped in Santander, Spain; GLASGOW was placed at Extended Readiness for a period in 2002; NOTTINGHAM was returned to UK after sustaining severe hull damage in Australia in late 2002. Her future is under consideration. The following decommissioning dates have been announced by the MoD: NEWCASTLE (2007), CARDIFF (2008); GLASGOW & LIVERPOOL (2010); EXETER (2011); SOUTHAMPTON and NOTTINGHAM (2012).

● DEREK FOX   **HMS Edinburgh**

SHEFFIELD CLASS
(Type 42) Batch 3

Ship	Pennant Number	Completion Date	Builder
MANCHESTER	D95	1983	Vickers
GLOUCESTER	D96	1984	Vosper T.
EDINBURGH	D97	1985	C. Laird
YORK	D98	1984	Swan Hunter

Displacement 4,775 tons **Dimensions** 132m x 15m x 7m **Speed** 30 knots + **Armament** 1- 4.5-inch gun, 2 - Phalanx, 2 - 20mm guns, Sea Dart missile system, Lynx Helicopter, 6 Torpedo Tubes **Complement** 269.

Notes
"Stretched' versions of earlier ships of this class. Designed to provide area defence of a task force. Deck edge stiffening fitted to counter increased hull stress. YORK conducted on board trial of Sea Ram inner layer missile defence system in 2001. This has since been removed. YORK and EDINBURGH (only) to be fitted with 4.5-inch Mod 1 gun. The MoD confirmed the following decommissioning dates: MANCHESTER & GLOUCESTER (2013), EDINBURGH & YORK (2014).

FRIGATES
DUKE CLASS (Type 23)

Ship	Pennant Number	Completion Date	Builder
KENT	F78	2000	Yarrow
PORTLAND	F79	2000	Yarrow
GRAFTON	F80	1996	Yarrow
SUTHERLAND	F81	1997	Yarrow
SOMERSET	F82	1996	Yarrow
ST ALBANS	F83	2001	Yarrow
LANCASTER	F229	1991	Yarrow
NORFOLK*	F230	1989	Yarrow
ARGYLL	F231	1991	Yarrow
MARLBOROUGH*	F233	1991	Swan Hunter
IRON DUKE*	F234	1992	Yarrow
MONMOUTH*	F235	1993	Yarrow
MONTROSE*	F236	1993	Yarrow
WESTMINSTER	F237	1993	Swan Hunter
NORTHUMBERLAND	F238	1994	Swan Hunter
RICHMOND	F239	1994	Swan Hunter

Displacement 3,500 tons **Dimensions** 133m x 15m x 5m **Speed** 28 knots **Armament** Harpoon & Seawolf missile systems: 1 - 4.5-inch gun, 2 - single 30mm guns, 4 - 2 twin, magazine launched, Torpedo Tubes, Lynx Helicopter (Merlin in LANCASTER) **Complement** 173.

Notes
These are now the backbone of the RN's frigate force. They incorporate 'Stealth' technology to minimise magnetic, radar, acoustic and infra-red signatures. Gas turbine and diesel electric propulsion. Those ships marked * will have been fitted with the Mk 8 Mod 1 4.5-inch gun by the end of 2003. The rest of class to be fitted by 2011.

HMS Portland

HMS Norfolk (complete with Mk8 4.5-inch Mod 1 gun)

HMS Cumberland

BROADSWORD CLASS
(Type 22) Batch 3

Ship	Pennant Number	Completion Date	Builder
CUMBERLAND	F85	1988	Yarrow
CAMPBELTOWN	F86	1988	C. Laird
CHATHAM	F87	1989	Swan Hunter
CORNWALL	F99	1987	Yarrow

Displacement 4,200 tons **Dimensions** 147m x 15m x 7m **Speed** 30 knots **Armament** 1 - 4.5-inch gun, 1 - Goalkeeper, 8 - Harpoon, 2 - Seawolf, 2 - 20mm guns, 6 Torpedo Tubes, 2 Lynx or 1 Sea King Helicopter **Complement** 259.

Notes
All these ships have an anti-submarine and intelligence gathering capability. All are capable of acting as fleet flagships. CUMBERLAND fitted with Mk8 4.5-inch Mod 1 gun in 2001 and remainder will be fitted by the end of the decade. SHEFFIELD, the last of the Batch 2 Type 22s, was prematurely withdrawn from service in October 2002. BRAVE and BOXER have been designated as future fleet targets.

HMS Middleton

MINE COUNTERMEASURES SHIPS (MCMV'S) HUNT CLASS

Ship	Pennant Number	Completion Date	Builder
BRECON	M29	1980	Vosper T.
LEDBURY	M30	1981	Vosper T.
CATTISTOCK	M31	1982	Vosper T.
COTTESMORE	M32	1983	Yarrow
BROCKLESBY	M33	1983	Vosper T.
MIDDLETON	M34	1984	Yarrow
DULVERTON	M35	1983	Vosper T.
CHIDDINGFOLD	M37	1984	Vosper T.
ATHERSTONE	M38	1987	Vosper T.
HURWORTH	M39	1985	Vosper T.
QUORN	M41	1989	Vosper T.

Displacement 625 tonnes **Dimensions** 60m x 10m x 2.2m **Speed** 17 knots **Armament** 1 x 30mm + 2 x 20mm guns **Complement** 42.

Notes
The largest warships ever built of glass reinforced plastic. Their cost (£35m each) has dictated the size of the class. Very sophisticated ships – and lively seaboats! All based at Portsmouth and Faslane. Ships are frequently deployed in the Fishery Protection role. COTTESMORE, BRECON and DULVERTON refitted as patrol boats for operations off Northern Ireland. Two of the class were sold to Greece in 2000 and 2001.

● MIKE WELSFORD

HMS Penzance

SANDOWN CLASS

Ship	Pennant Number	Completion Date	Builder
SANDOWN	M101	1989	Vosper T.
INVERNESS	M102	1991	Vosper T.
WALNEY	M104	1992	Vosper T.
BRIDPORT	M105	1993	Vosper T.
PENZANCE	M106	1998	Vosper T.
PEMBROKE	M107	1998	Vosper T.
GRIMSBY	M108	1999	Vosper T.
BANGOR	M109	2000	Vosper T.
RAMSEY	M110	2000	Vosper T.
BLYTH	M111	2001	Vosper T.
SHOREHAM	M112	2001	Vosper T.

Displacement 450 tons **Dimensions** 53m x 10m x 2m **Speed** 13 knots **Armament** 1 - 30mm gun **Complement** 34.

Notes
A class dedicated to a single mine hunting role. Propulsion is by vectored thrust and bow thrusters. CROMER paid off in 2001and was towed to Dartmouth in 2002 to become a static training hull (renamed HINDUSTAN). BRIDPORT is at Faslane in extended readiness. Her future is undecided.

HMS Dumbarton Castle

PATROL VESSELS
CASTLE CLASS

Ship	Pennant Number	Completion Date	Builder
LEEDS CASTLE	P258	1981	Hall Russell
DUMBARTON CASTLE	P265	1982	Hall Russell

Displacement 1,450 tons **Dimensions** 81m x 11m x 3m **Speed** 20 knots **Armament** 1 - 30mm gun **Complement** 42

Notes
These ships have a dual role – that of fishery protection and offshore patrols within the limits of UK territorial waters. Unlike the Island Class these ships are able to operate helicopters – including Sea King aircraft. LEEDS CASTLE is on long term deployment to the Falkland Islands with her ships' company rotating every four months. DUMBARTON CASTLE now has an MCM role.

HMS Tyne

RIVER CLASS

Ship	Pennant Number	Completion Date	Builder
TYNE	P281	2002	Vosper T.
SEVERN	P282	2003	Vosper T.
MERSEY	P283	2003	Vosper T.

Displacement 1700 tonnes **Dimensions** 80m x 13.5m x 3.8m **Speed** 20+ knots
Armament 1 x 20mm, 2 x GPMG **Complement** 48

Notes
Ordered on 8 May 2001, the deal is unusual in that the three ships are being leased from
Vospers for five years under a £60 million contract. Thereafter the opportunity exists for
the lease to be extended, the ships purchased outright or returned to Vospers. The contract also provides for Vospers to support and maintain the Island class whilst they
remain in service.

HMS Guernsey

ISLAND CLASS

Ship	Pennant Number	Completion Date	Builder
ANGLESEY	P277	1979	Hall Russell
GUERNSEY	P297	1977	Hall Russell
LINDISFARNE	P300	1978	Hall Russell

Displacement 1,250 tons **Dimensions** 60m x 11m x 4m **Speed** 17 knots
Armament 1 - 30mm gun **Complement** 37.

Notes
The last vessels of a class of seven. Built on trawler lines these ships were introduced to protect the extensive British interests in North Sea oil/gas installations and to patrol the 200 mile fishery limit. All vessels have extra crew members to allow leave to be taken and thus extend vessels time on task over the year. SHETLAND and ALDERNEY paid off in 2002 and were sold to Bangladesh. The remaining three vessels will follow in 2003 as the River class are delivered.

COASTAL TRAINING CRAFT
P2000 CLASS

Ship	Pennant Number	Completion Date	Builder
EXPRESS	P163	1988	Vosper T.
EXPLORER	P164	1985	Watercraft
EXAMPLE	P165	1985	Watercraft
EXPLOIT	P167	1988	Vosper T.
ARCHER	P264	1985	Watercraft
BITER	P270	1985	Watercraft
SMITER	P272	1986	Watercraft
PURSUER	P273	1988	Vosper T.
TRACKER	P274	1998	Ailsa Troon
RAIDER	P275	1998	Ailsa Troon
BLAZER	P279	1988	Vosper T.
DASHER	P280	1988	Vosper T.
PUNCHER	P291	1988	Vosper T.
CHARGER	P292	1988	Vosper T.
RANGER	P293	1988	Vosper T.
TRUMPETER	P294	1988	Vosper T.

Displacement 43 tonnes **Dimensions** 20m x 6m x 1m **Speed** 20 knots **Armament** 1 x GPMG (TRUMPETER and RANGER only) **Complement** 5 (with accommodation for up to 12 undergraduates).

Notes
In service with RN University units (URNU) as training vessels. TRUMPETER and RANGER deployed to Gibraltar in 1991 and armed in 2002. They are expected to return to the UK in 2003. Former Example Class Training vessels were operated by the RNXS - until the organisation was disbanded on 31 March 1994. Vessels were then transferred to RN University Units as sea training tenders. Vessels are assigned to the following URNUs: ARCHER (Aberdeen); BITER (Manchester); BLAZER (Southampton); CHARGER (Liverpool); DASHER (Bristol); EXAMPLE (Northumbria); EXPLOIT (Birmingham); EXPLORER (Yorkshire); EXPRESS (Wales); PUNCHER (London); PURSUER (Sussex); RAIDER (Cambridge); SMITER (Glasgow); TRACKER (Oxford).

● DANIEL FERRO

HMS Trumpeter

HMS Example

● DAVE CULLEN

LPV Greyfox

LIFESPAN PATROL VESSELS (Lpvs)

Ship	Pennant Number	Completion Date	Builder
GREYFOX		1988	Halmatic
GREYWOLF		1988	Halmatic

Displacement 18.5 tons **Dimensions** 16m x 4.7m x 1.4m **Speed** 27+ knots
Armament Nil **Complement** 4

Notes
Purpose built in 1988 for counter terrorism duties on Lough Neagh, Northern Ireland.
Operated in anonimity until withdrawn from service in 2002, following a review of RN
operations in the Province. Transferred to Gibraltar in September 2002 to join the
Gibraltar Patrol Squadron. Are likely to replace TRUMPETER and RANGER once fully
worked up. The new vessels are more capable than the P2000s in speed, armoured
areas and surveillance equipment. Can transport more than 30 passengers for short
periods. GREYFOX appears to have a FLIR turret on the bridge roof. If trials are successful the craft will be commissioned as "White Ensign" vessels and operate with an
RN crew.

● CHRIS ROGERS

HMS Scott

SURVEY SHIPS

Ship	Pennant Number	Completion Date	Builder
SCOTT	H 131	1997	Appledore

Displacement 13,300 tonnes **Dimensions** 130m x 21.5m x 14m **Speed** 17 knots
Complement 63

Notes
SCOTT carries a mixture of the latest UK and US survey equipment. The sonar system is US supplied. She operates a three watch system whereby the vessel is run by 42 of the ships company of 63 with the remainder on leave. Each crew member works 75 days in the ship before having 30 days off, allowing her to spend more than 300 days at sea in a year. These manpower reductions over previous survey ships have been possible because of the extensive use of commercial lean manning methods including unmanned machinery spaces, fixed fire fighting systems and extensive machinery and safety surveillance technology.

● WALTER SARTORI

HMS Echo

ECHO CLASS

Ship	Pennant Number	Completion Date	Builder
ECHO	H 87	2002	Appledore
ENTERPRISE	H 88	2003	Appledore

Displacement 3,470 tonnes **Dimensions** 90m x 16.8m x 5.5.m **Speed** 15 knots **Complement** 46 (with accommodation for 81)

Notes

In June 2000, a £130 million order was placed with prime contractor Vosper Thornycroft to build and maintain, over a 25 year period, two new Survey Vessels Hydrographic Oceanographic (SVHO). Both vessels were built by sub-contractor Appledore Shipbuilding Limited. They have a secondary role as mine countermeasures flag ships. ECHO was handed over in September 2002. ENTERPRISE is scheduled to be handed over in March 2003 with an Operational Date of July 2003. They will be operationally available for 330 days a year. Utilizing a diesel electric propulsion system, they have three main generators. They are the first RN ships to be fitted with Azimuth thrusters in place of the more normal shaft and propellor.

● DAVID HANNAFORD

HMS Roebuck

Ship	Pennant Number	Completion Date	Builder
ROEBUCK	H130	1986	Brooke Marine

Displacement 1500 tonnes **Dimensions** 64m x 13m x 4m **Speed** 15 knots **Complement** 51.

Notes

Able to operate for long periods away from shore support, this ship and the other vessels of the Hydrographic Fleet collect the data that is required to produce the Admiralty Charts and publications which are sold to mariners worldwide. Fitted with the latest fixing aids and sector scanning sonar. Scheduled to pay-off in April 2003.

• I. PORTER

HMS Gleaner

INSHORE SURVEY VESSEL

Ship	Pennant Number	Completion Date	Builder
GLEANER	H86	1983	Emsworth

Displacement 22 tons **Dimensions** 14.8m x 4.7m x 1.3m **Speed** 14 knots
Complement 5.

Notes
Small inshore survey craft used for the collection of data from the shallowest inshore waters. Will remain in service until at least 2007.

• DEREK FOX

HMS Endurance

ICE PATROL SHIP

Ship	Pennant Number	Completion Date	Builder
ENDURANCE	A171	1990	Ulstein-Hatlo

Displacement 5,129 tons **Dimensions** 91m x 17.9m x 6.5m **Speed** 14.9 knots
Armament Small arms **Aircraft** 2 Lynx **Complement** 116

Notes
Chartered for only 7 months in late 1991 to replace the older vessel of the same name. Originally M/V POLAR CIRCLE, renamed HMS POLAR CIRCLE (A176) and then purchased by MOD(N) and renamed again in October 1992 to current name. Spends 4-6 months each year in the South Atlantic supporting the British Antarctic Survey. Will remain in service until at least 2015.

33

RV Triton

RESEARCH VESSEL

Ship	Pennant Number	Completion Date	Builder
TRITON	-	2000	Vosper Thornycroft

Displacement 1,100 tons **Dimensions** 98m x 22.5m x 3.2m **Speed** 20 knots
Complement 12 crew + 12 scientific personnel

Notes

Operated by QinetiQ (formerly DERA) the vessel is a two third scale demonstrator described as the most significant advance in naval design since the Dreadnoughts. The vessel is being used to explore the potential of the advanced trimaran hull form. If successful, the design could form the basis of the Future Surface Combattant.

SHIPS FOR THE FUTURE FLEET...

ASTUTE - The In Service Date (ISD) for ASTUTE has now slipped, approximately by a further 18 months. This is due to slow progress in the detailed design and in the build up of production. The submarine had been expected to enter service in June 2005, however, she is not now expected to enter service before late 2006. In addition, ASTUTE will have to undergo considerable trials and work-up before she becomes fully operational. The MoD has not disclosed the dates when AMBUSH and ARTFUL will enter service.

TYPE 45 - With a class of up to twelve ships planned, the Government has presently ordered six. The first of the class will be assembled and launched at Scotstoun (formerly Yarrow). All remaining ships will be assembled and launched at Barrow. Construction will involve pre-fabricated methods. The work will be divided between BAE Systems at Govan and Scotstoun and Vosper Thornycroft. DARING is scheduled to enter service in 2007, followed by DAUNTLESS and DIAMOND in 2009. DRAGON, DEFENDER and DUNCAN will follow in 2010 and 2011. The cost of the first six ships is expected to be about £4.3 billion, including research and development.

ALTERNATIVE LANDING SHIPS LOGISTIC - An intention to order four ALSLs, to be operated by the RFA, was announced in October 2000. Based on the Dutch ROTTERDAM LPD design. The first two, LYME BAY and LARGS BAY are being built by Swan Hunter on the Tyne. First steel was cut in October 2001. The contract for the second two, placed with BAE Systems, was signed in November 2001. These ships, to be named MOUNTS BAY and CARDIGAN BAY, will be constructed at Govan. They will replace four of the five ships of the Sir Class. With a tonnage of 16,160 tonnes they will be substantially bigger than the ships they replace. On joining the fleet, to more accurately reflect their design and role, they will be designated Auxiliary LSDs (LSD(A)).

FUTURE CARRIER PROGRAMME (CVF) - The Royal Navy and Royal Air Force are to receive up to 150 Short Take Off and Vertical Landing (STOVL) versions of the new Lockheed Martin F35 Joint Strike Fighter, which MoD has chosen as having the best potential to replace both land-based and carrier-based Harrier aircraft, in a programme worth up to £10 billion. They will enter service with the first of the new carriers in 2012.

The aircraft carriers are to displace between 50,000 and 60,000 tonnes but would be initially configured for STOVL operations and be fitted with a ski-jump. The carriers are expected to have a life of 50 years and therefore the design of the ship will allow for the installation of catapults and arrestor gear to operate any later generation of aircraft which may succeed the JCA. The current decision to opt for STOVL operations also indicates that the RN will continue to rely on rotary wing Airborne Early Warning for the forseeable future.

The overall cost of acquiring and operating the JCA over a 25 year period will be around £10 billion, whilst the two aircraft carriers are expected to cost around £3 billion.

Selection of the prime contractor for the CVF programme, either Thales or BAE Systems is expected to be announced early in 2003. Both consortia announced their build strategies at the end of 2002. Both involve prefabricated construction of 3-5 "megablocks" and both have indicated Rosyth as their preferred site for final assembly.

THE ROYAL FLEET AUXILIARY

The Royal Fleet Auxiliary Service (RFA) is a civilian manned fleet owned and operated by the Ministry of Defence. Its main task is to supply warships of the Royal Navy at sea with fuel, food, stores and ammunition which they need to remain operational while away from base. The service also provides aviation support and training facilities for the Royal Navy – together with amphibious support and secure sea transport for for the Royal Marines and British Army units.

The RFA is the largest single employer of UK merchant navy officers and ratings. Although the ethos is very much based on that of the Merchant Service, the personnel undergo a considerable overlay of naval training, in the main to provide them with a greater degree of survivability when operating their ships in hostile waters. Such training includes the operation and maintenance of close range and small calibre weapons and decoys (self-defence weapons), firefighting and damage control. But, fundamental to the success of the RFA is the need for competent seamen to undertake replenishment at sea and small boat operations, and to man ships flight decks to ensure the safe operation of helicopters.

The service prides itself that each ship is available for operations for approximately 80% of the year. Unlike the Royal Navy, officers and men of the RFA join a vessel for a period of time - say six months - and do not expect to be in port for leave periods at all during this period.

As 2002 arrived, the small RFA Fleet was continuing to provide round the clock support to frontline warships deployed around the world. The seven tankers have been on station in the South Atlantic, Caribbean, Indian Ocean and Persian Gulf throughout the year, whilst the stores ships have accompanied Carrier groups and Amphibious groups wherever they deploy, always on hand to provide fuel, food, ammunition and spares as required.

The year also saw the return of RFA SIR GERAINT. She arrived back in the UK in August after having spent 15 months alongside in Freetown, Sierra Leone, in support of ongoing stabilisation efforts in the country.

Strain on the ever ageing RFA fleet, caused by the demands of high tempo RN operations and deployments, will be eased in 2003 with the arrival of some much needed new tonnage. Both WAVE KNIGHT and WAVE RULER were handed over by BAE Systems at the end of 2002, finally conferring on the RFA again a fast tanker capability, something that had been lacking since the disposal of the old steam driven "O" class tankers at the end of the 1990s.

SHIPS OF THE ROYAL FLEET AUXILIARY
Pennant Numbers

Ship	Pennant Number	Ship	Pennant Number	Ship	Pennant Number
BRAMBLELEAF	A81	GREY ROVER	A269	WAVE KNIGHT	A389
SEA CRUSADER	A96	GOLD ROVER	A271	WAVE RULER	A390
BAYLEAF	A109	BLACK ROVER	A273	SIR BEDIVERE	L3004
ORANGELEAF	A110	FORT ROSALIE	A385	SIR GALAHAD	L3005
OAKLEAF	A111	FORT AUSTIN	A386	SIR GERAINT	L3027
DILIGENCE	A132	FORT VICTORIA	A387	SIR PERCIVALE	L3036
ARGUS	A135	FORT GEORGE	A388	SIR TRISTRAM	L3505

KEEP UP TO DATE THROUGHOUT THE YEAR

Warship World is published six times a year (Jan, Mar, May, Jul, Sep, Nov) and gives you all the information necessary to keep this book updated throughout the year.

RFA Wave Knight

FLEET TANKERS
WAVE CLASS

Ship	Pennant Number	Completion Date	Builder
WAVE KNIGHT	A 389	2002	BAE Systems
WAVE RULER	A 390	2002	BAE Systems

Displacement 30,300 tons (Full Load) **Dimensions** 196 x 27 x 10m **Speed** 18 knots
Armament 2 x Vulcan Phalanx (fitted for but not with), 2 x 30mm **Aircraft** 1 Merlin
Complement 80 (plus 22 Fleet Air Arm)

Notes
A new class of Fast Fleet Support Tankers to replace the two O class vessels sold for scrap in 2000. WAVE KNIGHT was eventually handed over from the builders at the end of September 2002. WAVE RULER was launched in February 2001 at Govan, and was handed over from the builders in October 2002.

RFA Oakleaf

SUPPORT TANKERS

Ship	Pennant Number	Completion Date	Builder
OAKLEAF	A111	1981	Uddevalla

Displacement 49,310 tons **Dimensions** 173.7m x 32.2m x 11.2m **Speed** 14 knots **Complement** 35.

Notes

At 49,310 tons displacement, she is the largest vessel in RN/RFA service. Her role, along with other support tankers, is to provide the fuel vital to enable the Navy's warships to operate far from their UK bases.

RFA Brambleleaf

LEAF CLASS

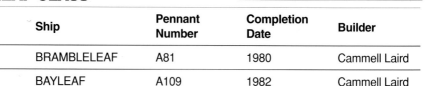

Ship	Pennant Number	Completion Date	Builder
BRAMBLELEAF	A81	1980	Cammell Laird
BAYLEAF	A109	1982	Cammell Laird
ORANGELEAF	A110	1982	Cammell Laird

Displacement 37,747 tons **Dimensions** 170m x 26m x 12m **Speed** 14.5 knots **Complement** 60.

Notes
All are ex merchant ships, originally acquired for employment mainly on freighting duties. All have been modified to enable them to refuel warships at sea. One of the class is normally permanently on station in the Gulf in support of Armilla Patrol and allied warships. BRAMBLELEAF is MoD(N) owned, the remainder on long-term bareboat charter. All are commercial Stat32 class tankers.

RFA Grey Rover

ROVER CLASS

Ship	Pennant Number	Completion Date	Builder
GREY ROVER	A269	1970	Swan Hunter
GOLD ROVER	A271	1974	Swan Hunter
BLACK ROVER	A273	1974	Swan Hunter

Displacement 11,522 tons **Dimensions** 141m x 19m x 7m **Speed** 18 knots **Armament** 2 - 20mm guns **Complement** 49/54

Notes
Small Fleet Tankers designed to supply warships with fresh water, dry cargo and refrigerated provisions, as well as a range of fuels and lubricants. Helicopter deck, but no hangar. Have been employed in recent years mainly as support for HM Ships operating around the Falkland Islands and West Indies, spending up to two years on deployment in these areas. There are currently no plans to replace these three ships before 2007.

RFA Fort Austin

STORES VESSELS
FORT CLASS I

Ship	Pennant Number	Completion Date	Builder
FORT ROSALIE	A385	1978	Scott Lithgow
FORT AUSTIN	A386	1979	Scott Lithgow

Displacement 23,384 tons **Dimensions** 183m x 24m x 9m **Speed** 20 knots **Complement** 201, (120 RFA, 36 MoD Civilians & 45 Fleet Air Arm).

Notes
Full hangar and maintenance facilities are provided and up to four Sea King helicopters can be carried for both the transfer of stores and anti-submarine protection of a group of ships. Both ships can be armed with 4 - 20mm guns.

● DAVE CULLEN

RFA Fort Victoria

REPLENISHMENT SHIPS
FORT CLASS II

Ship	Pennant Number	Completion Date	Builder
FORT VICTORIA	A387	1992	Harland & Wolff
FORT GEORGE	A388	1993	Swan Hunter

Displacement 31,500 tons **Dimensions** 204m x 30m x 9m **Speed** 20 knots **Armament** 4 - 30mm guns, 2 x Phalanx CIWS, Sea Wolf Missile System (Fitted for but not with) **Complement** 100 (RFA), 24 MoD Civilians, 32 RN and up to 122 Fleet Air Arm.

Notes

"One stop" replenishment ships with the widest range of armaments, fuel and spares carried. Can operate up to 5 Sea King Helicopters with full maintenance facilities onboard. Flight deck facilities frequently used as training area for helicopter crews. Medical facilities were upgraded in 2001 to give the vessels a limited role as Primary Casualty Receiving Ships.

• DEREK FOX

RFA Sir Bedivere

LANDING SHIPS (LOGISTIC) SIR CLASS

Ship	Pennant Number	Completion Date	Builder
SIR BEDIVERE	L3004	1967	Hawthorn
SIR GALAHAD	L3005	1987	Swan Hunter
SIR GERAINT	L3027	1967	Stephen
SIR PERCIVALE	L3036	1968	Hawthorn
SIR TRISTRAM	L3505	1967	Hawthorn

Displacement 5,550 tons **Dimensions** 126m x 18m x 4m **Speed** 17 knots **Armament** Can be fitted with 20 or 40mm guns in emergency **Complement** 65, (SIR GALAHAD is larger at 8,451 tons. 140m x 20m **Complement** 58)

Notes
Manned by the RFA but tasked by the Commodore Amphibious Task Group (COMATG), these ships are used for heavy secure transport of stores – embarked by bow and stern doors. Can operate helicopters from both vehicle and flight deck if required and carry 340 troops. SIR TRISTRAM was rebuilt after extensive Falklands War damage. After extensive delays, SIR BEDIVERE completed a Ship Life Extension Programme (SLEP) at Rosyth in 1998. She is now 7,700 tonnes displacement and her dimensions are 137 x 20 x 4 metres. Occasionally used for MCMV support. SIR GERAINT at extended readiness since September 2002. Her future has yet to be decided.

RFA Sea Crusader

RO-RO VESSEL

Ship	Pennant Number	Completion Date	Builder
SEA CRUSADER	A96	1996	Kawasaki Heavy Industries

Displacement 25,500 tonnes **Dimensions** 164m x 25m x 6.5m **Speed** 18 knots
Complement 17

Notes
A commercial Roll on-Roll off cargo ship, chartered while under construction in Japan. Arrived in UK in November 1996, her main role being a heavy-lift ship for the Joint Rapid Reaction Force. Routinely employed on freighting runs transporting armoured vehicles and equipment to the Mediterranean, and continental ports. 2,500 lane metres of vehicle capacity available. Originally due to be returned to her owners in October 1998 her MoD charter has, however, once again been extended until March 2003. A similar vessel, SEA CENTURION, was returned to her owners in August 2002.

● CHRIS ROGERS

RFA Diligence

FORWARD REPAIR SHIP

Ship	Pennant Number	Completion Date	Builder
DILIGENCE	A132	1981	Oesundsvarvet

Displacement 5,814 tons **Dimensions** 120m x 12m x 3m **Speed** 15 knots **Armament** 2 - 20mm **Complement** RFA 40, RN Personnel – approx 100.

Notes
Formerly the M/V STENA INSPECTOR purchased (£25m) for service in the South Atlantic. Her deep diving complex was removed and workshops added. When not employed on "battle repair" duties can serve as support vessel for MCMVs and submarines on deployment.

46

RFA Argus

AVIATION TRAINING SHIP

Ship	Pennant Number	Completion Date	Builder
ARGUS	A135	1981	Cantieri Navali Breda

Displacement 28,081 tons (full load) **Dimensions** 175m x 30m x 8m **Speed** 18 knots
Armament 4 - 30 mm, 2 - 20 mm **Complement** 254 (inc 137 Fleet Air Arm)
Aircraft 6 Sea King/Merlin, 12 Harriers can be carried in a "ferry role".

Notes
Formerly the M/V CONTENDER BEZANT taken up from trade during the Falklands crisis. Purchased in 1984 (£13 million) for conversion to an 'Aviation Training Ship'. A £50 million re-build was undertaken at Belfast from 1984-87. Undertook rapid conversion in October 1990 to Primary Casualty Reception Ship for service in the Gulf. These facilities were upgraded and made permanent during 2001.

47

• WALTER SARTORI

MV Hurst Point

STRATEGIC SEALIFT RO-RO VESSELS

Ship	Pennant Number	Completion Date	Builder
HURST POINT		2002	Flensburger
HARTLAND POINT		2002	Harland & Wolff
EDDYSTONE		2002	Flensburger
LONGSTONE		2003	Flensburger
ANVIL POINT		2003	Harland & Wolff
BEACHY HEAD		2003	Flensburger

Displacement 20,000 tonnes, **Dimensions** 193m x 26m x 6.6m **Speed** 18 knots **Complement** 38

Notes
The contract for the supply of six ro-ro vessels to meet the requirements for stategic sealift capabilities was announced in October 2000. Under a 25 year private finance initiative deal, AWSR Shipping Limited were contracted to build and run the vessels for the MoD. The contract, likely to be worth up to £950 million, was finally signed on 27 June 2002. The MoD will normally use four of the ships, with all six available for operations. The unarmed ships have green hulls, white superstructure, yellow funnels and fly the Red Ensign.

HMS GLOUCESTER and RFA GOLD ROVER

MoD/Crown Copyright

HM Ships SOUTHAMPTON (front) and CORNWALL

BAE Systems

RFA WAVE RULER

HM Ships ILLUSTRIOUS and CORNWALL

ORANGELEAF
LONDON

A110

MoD/Crown Copyright

RFA ORANGELEAF

HMS HURWORTH

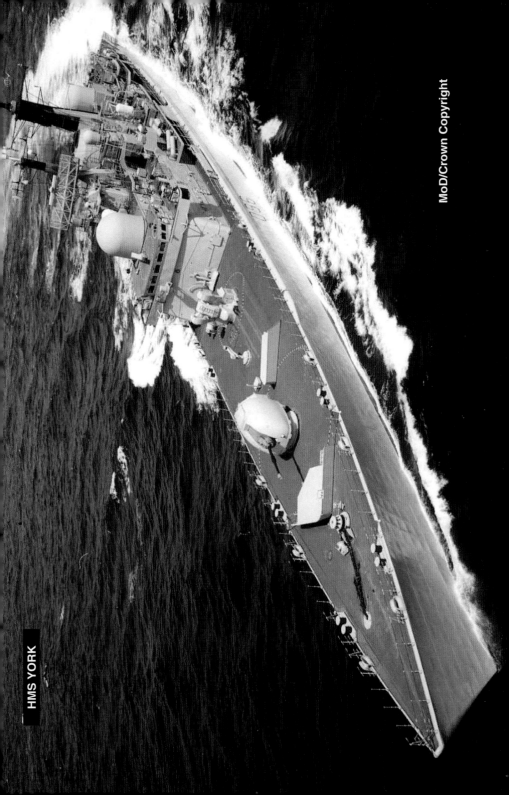

HMS YORK

MoD/Crown Copyright

Two of the RN's newest frigates, KENT & PORTLAND, hand over duties in the Persian Gulf.

MARINE SERVICES SUPPORT

The Chief Executive Warship Support Agency (WSA) is tasked by the Defence Logistic Organisation (DLO) with Tri-Service provision of Marine Services and is responsible for In and Out-of-Port maritime services in support of Naval Bases, CinC Fleet, The Meteorological Office, QinetiQ (formerly DERA), RAF and Army. Their role is to undertake Mooring and Navigation buoy maintenance, freighting of Naval armaments and explosives, maritime support to the underwater research programme and sea-borne services to the Fleet. Maritime services at the Kyle of Lochalsh are provided primarily to support the BUTEC Ranges, and secondarily to fulfil Fleet requirements in that area.

In the three main Ports at Portsmouth, Devonport and Clyde the service is currently delivered under a Government Owned/Commercially Operated (GOCO) contract with SERCo-Denholm Ltd. The vessels being operated on a BARECON (Bareboat charter) basis.

For Naval Armament Freighting, Mooring Maintenance, RMAS NEWTON and services at Kyle of Lochalsh, the service is currently delivered by the General Manager RMAS from his HQ at Pembroke Dock.

For both RAF training and Range Safety Clearance duties at Army and MoD ranges throughout Britain, services are currently delivered under two separate Government Owned/Commercially Operated (GOCO) contracts. The Ministry was still in negotiation in 2002 with industry to bring these operations under one new contract.

Marine Services vessels can be seen at work in the UK Naval Bases and are easily identified by their black hulls, buff coloured superstructure and by their Flag, which in the case of GM RMAS vessels, is a blue ensign defaced in the fly by a yellow anchor over two wavy lines. The remaining vessels fly the 'Other Government' ensign. Which is a blue ensign defaced in the fly by a yellow anchor.

SHIPS OF
THE MARINE SERVICES
Pennant Numbers

Ship	Pennant Number	Page	Ship	Pennant Number	Page
CAMERON	A72	78	POWERFUL	A223	60
MELTON	A83	73	ADEPT	A224	60
MENAI	A84	73	BUSTLER	A225	60
MEON	A87	73	CAPABLE	A226	60
DALMATIAN	A129	61	CAREFUL	A227	60
TORNADO	A140	76	FAITHFUL	A228	60
TORMENTOR	A142	76	COL. TEMPLER	A229	65
WATERMAN	A146	75	DEXTEROUS	A231	60
FRANCES	A147	63	ADAMANT	A232	72
FLORENCE	A149	63	SHEEPDOG	A250	61
GENEVIEVE	A150	63	LADYBIRD	A253	67
KITTY	A170	62	NEWHAVEN	A280	69
LESLEY	A172	62	NUTBOURNE	A281	69
HUSKY	A178	61	NETLEY	A282	69
SALUKI	A182	61	OBAN	A283	70
SALMOOR	A185	77	ORONSAY	A284	70
SALMAID	A187	77	OMAGH	A285	70
SETTER	A189	61	PADSTOW	A286	71
JOAN	A190	62	IMPULSE	A344	59
BOVISAND	A191	68	IMPETUS	A345	59
CAWSAND	A192	68	NEWTON	A367	64
HELEN	A198	63	WARDEN	A368	79
MYRTLE	A199	62	KINTERBURY	A378	66
SPANIEL	A201	61	OILPRESS	Y21	74
NORAH	A205	61	MOORHEN	Y32	78
FORCEFUL	A221	60	MOORFOWL	Y33	78
NIMBLE	A222	60			

MV Impetus

TUGS

IMPULSE CLASS

Ship	Pennant Number	Completion Date	Builder
IMPULSE	A344	1993	R. Dunston
IMPETUS	A345	1993	R. Dunston

G.R.T. 400 tons approx **Dimensions** 33m x 10m x 4m **Speed** 12 knots **Complement** 5.

Notes
Completed in 1993 specifically to serve as berthing tugs for the Trident Class submarines at Faslane. Both operated under contract by Serco Denholm.

• DONALD DONALDSON   **MV Dexterous**

TWIN UNIT TRACTOR TUGS (TUTT'S)

Ship	Pennant Number	Completion Date	Builder
FORCEFUL	A221	1985	R. Dunston
NIMBLE	A222	1985	R. Dunston
POWERFUL	A223	1985	R. Dunston
ADEPT	A224	1980	R. Dunston
BUSTLER	A225	1981	R. Dunston
CAPABLE	A226	1981	R. Dunston
CAREFUL	A227	1982	R. Dunston
FAITHFUL	A228	1985	R. Dunston
DEXTEROUS	A231	1986	R. Dunston

G.R.T. 375 tons **Dimensions** 39m x 10m x 4m **Speed** 12 knots **Complement** 9.

Notes
The principal harbour tugs in naval service. All operated under contract by Serco Denholm except CAPABLE at Gibraltar which is managed locally.

MV Husky

DOG CLASS

Ship	Pennant Number	Completion Date	Builder
DALMATION	A129	1965	J.S. Doig
HUSKY	A178	1969	Appledore
SALUKI	A182	1969	Appledore
SETTER	A189	1969	Appledore
SHEEPDOG	A250	1969	Appledore
SPANIEL	A201	1967	Appledore

G.R.T. 152 tons **Dimensions** 29m x 8m x 4m **Speed** 12 knots **Complement** 5.

Notes
General harbour tugs – all completed between 1965 and 1969. COLLIE and CAIRN replaced at Kyle of Lochalsh by civilian vessels under charter to MoD during 2001. MASTIFF sold for commercial service.

MV Kitty

TRITON CLASS

Ship	Pennant Number	Completion Date	Builder
KITTY	A170	1972	R. Dunston
LESLEY	A172	1973	R. Dunston
JOAN	A190	1972	R. Dunston
MYRTLE	A199	1973	R. Dunston
NORAH	A205	1973	R. Dunston

G.R.T. 89 tons **Speed** 8 knots **Complement** 4.

Notes

Known as Water Tractors these craft are used for basin moves and towage of light barges. Operated by Serco Denholm Ltd. LILAH sold 2001.

MV Florence

FELICITY CLASS

Ship	Pennant Number	Completion Date	Builder
FLORENCE	A149	1980	R. Dunston
FRANCES	A147	1980	R. Dunston
GENEVIEVE	A150	1980	R. Dunston
HELEN	A198	1974	R. Dunston

G.R.T. 80 tons **Speed** 10 knots **Complement** 4.

Notes
Water Tractors used for the movement of small barges and equipment. All are operated by Serco Denholm. Two sister vessels (GEORGINA and GWENDOLINE) sold to Serco Denholm in 1996 for service in H M Naval bases. FIONA for sale 2002.

RMAS Newton

RESEARCH VESSELS

Ship	Pennant Number	Completion Date	Builder
NEWTON	A367	1976	Scotts

G.R.T. 2,779 tons **Dimensions** 99m x 16m x 6m **Speed** 15 knots **Complement** 27

Notes
Primarily used in the support of RN training exercises. Some limited support provided for various trials. Operated by the RMAS. Completed major refit in 2001 to extend life. Is frequently seen with Royal Marine small craft embarked.

• DONALD DONALDSON

MV Colonel Templer

Ship	Pennant Number	Completion Date	Builder
COLONEL TEMPLER A 229		1966	Hall Russell

Displacement 1,300 tons **Dimensions** 56m x 11m x 5.6 m **Speed** 12 knots
Complement 14

Notes

Built as a stern trawler but converted in 1980 for use by the Defence Evaluation and Research Agency as an acoustic research vessel. A major rebuild was completed after a serious fire gutted the ship in 1990. 12 scientists can be carried. From Nov 2000 operated on the Clyde by Serco Denholm. Used in support of trials and converted in 2001 to support RN diving training vice IXWORTH and IRONBRIDGE.

RMAS Kinterbury

NAVAL ARMAMENT VESSELS

Ship	Pennant Number	Completion Date	Builder
KINTERBURY	A378	1981	Appledore SB

G.R.T. 1,357 tons **Dimensions** 64m x 12m x 5m **Speed** 14 knots **Complement** 11.

Notes
Two holds carry Naval armament stores, ammunition and guided missiles. In addition to freighting tasks it is also used for trials work and in support of RN exercises.

MV Ladybird

ARMAMENT CARRIER

Ship	Pennant Number	Completion Date	Builder
LADYBIRD	A253	1973	Beverley

G.R.T. 279 tons **Dimensions** 34m x 8m x 3m **Speed** 10.5 knots **Complement** 7-9.

Notes
A Naval Armament carrier operated by Serco Denholm. BEE was for sale in late 2001.

MV Cawsand

TENDERS
STORM CLASS

Ship	Pennant Number	Completion Date	Builder
BOVISAND	A191	1997	FBM (Cowes)
CAWSAND	A192	1997	FBM (Cowes)

G.R.T 225 tonnes **Dimensions** 23m x 11m x 2m **Speed** 15 knots **Complement** 5

Notes

These craft are used in support of Flag Officer Sea Training (FOST) at Plymouth to transfer staff quickly and comfortably to and from Warships and Auxiliaries within and beyond the Plymouth breakwater in open sea conditions. These are the first vessels of a small waterplane area twin hull (SWATH) design to be ordered by the Ministry of Defence and cost £6.5 million. Speed restrictions implemented due to wash problems.

MV Nutbourne

NEWHAVEN CLASS

Ship	Pennant Number	Completion Date	Builder
NEWHAVEN	A280	2000	Aluminium SB
NUTBOURNE	A281	2000	Aluminium SB
NETLEY	A282	2001	Aluminium SB

Tonnage 77 tonnes (45 grt) **Dimensions** 18.3m x 6.8m x 1.88m **Speed** 10 knots **Complement** 3 Crew (60 passengers).

Notes
MCA Class IV Passenger Vessels based at Portsmouth. Replacements for Fleet tenders. Employed on general passenger duties.

MV Oransay

OBAN CLASS

Ship	Pennant Number	Completion Date	Builder
OBAN	A283	2000	McTay
ORONSAY	A284	2000	McTay
OMAGH	A285	2000	McTay

Tonnage 199 tons **Dimensions** 27.7m x 7.30m x 3.75m **Speed** 10 knots **Complement** 5 Crew (60 passengers).

Notes
New MCA Class IIA Passenger Vessels to replace Fleet tenders. Employed on general passenger duties on the Clyde.

MV Padstow

PADSTOW CLASS

Ship	Pennant Number	Completion Date	Builder
PADSTOW	A286	2000	Aluminium SB

Tonnage 77 tonnes (45 grt) **Dimensions** 18.3m x 6.8m x 1.88m **Speed** 10 knots **Complement** 3 Crew (60 passengers).

Notes
MCA Class VIA Passenger Vessel based at Plymouth. Used on general passenger ferrying duties and in support of FOST seariders.

MV Adamant

PERSONNEL FERRY

Ship	Pennant Number	Completion Date	Builder
ADAMANT	A232	1992	FBM (Cowes)

G.R.T 170 tonnes **Dimensions** 30m x 8m x 1m **Speed** 22 knots **Complement** 5

Notes

Twin catamaran hulls based on the commercial Red Jet design (as used by Red Funnel Ferry Co). First water jet propulsion vessel owned by MoD(N). In service as a Clyde personnel ferry - operated by Serco Denholm.

MV Menai

FLEET TENDERS

Ship	Pennant Number	Completion Date	Builder
MELTON	A83	1981	Richard Dunston
MENAI	A84	1981	Richard Dunston
MEON	A87	1982	Richard Dunston

G.R.T. 78 tons **Dimensions** 24m x 6m x 3m **Speed** 10.5 knots **Complement** 4/5.

Notes

The last three survivors of a once numerous class of tender used as Training Tenders, Passenger Ferries, or Cargo Vessels. MENAI and MEON are operated by Serco Denholm. IRONBRIDGE, INSTOW, ILCHESTER and IXWORTH were withdrawn from service in November 2002.

● DONALD DONALDSON

MV Oilpress

COASTAL OILER

Ship	Pennant Number	Completion Date	Builder
OILPRESS	Y21	1969	Appledore Shipbuilders

G.R.T. 362 tons **Dimensions** 41m x 9m x 3m **Speed** 11 knots **Complement** 5.

Notes
Employed as Harbour and Coastal Oiler. Operated by Serco Denholm on the Clyde.

MV Waterman

WATER CARRIER

Ship	Pennant Number	Completion Date	Builder
WATERMAN	A146	1978	R. Dunston

G.R.T. 263 tons **Dimensions** 40m x 8m x 2m **Speed** 11 knots **Complement** 5.

Notes
Capable of coastal passages, but normally supplies either demineralised or fresh water to the Fleet within port limits. WATERFOWL is owned and operated by Serco Denholm.

MV Tormentor

TORPEDO RECOVERY VESSELS (TRV)
TORNADO CLASS

Ship	Pennant Number	Completion Date	Builder
TORNADO	A140	1979	Hall Russell
TORMENTOR	A142	1980	Hall Russell

G.R.T. 560 tons **Dimensions** 47m x 8m x 3m **Speed** 14 knots **Complement** 13.

Notes
All vessels have had suitable rails fitted to enable them to operate as exercise minelayers. Converted in 2002 to support RN diving training (in lieu of Fleet Tenders) in addition to their other roles.

76

RMAS Salmaid

MOORING & SALVAGE VESSELS
SAL CLASS

Ship	Pennant Number	Completion Date	Builder
SALMOOR	A185	1985	Hall Russell
SALMAID	A187	1986	Hall Russell

Displacement 2,200 tonnes **Dimensions** 77m x 15m x 4m **Speed** 15 knots **Complement** 19

Notes
Multi-purpose vessels designed to lay and maintain underwater targets, navigation marks and moorings.

MV Moorhen

MOOR CLASS

Ship	Pennant Number	Completion Date	Builder
MOORHEN	Y32	1989	McTay Marine
MOORFOWL	Y33	1989	McTay Marine
CAMERON	A72	1991	Richard Dunston

Displacement 518 tons **Dimensions** 32m x 11m x 2m **Speed** 8 knots **Complement** 10

Notes
Powered mooring lighters for use within sheltered coastal waters. CAMERON is similar but was sold to DERA at Dunfermline in 1996 and is employed as an Underwater Trials & Experimental vessel at Rosyth. Operated by Briggs Marine on behalf of QinetiQ. MOORHEN based at Portsmouth and MOORFOWL at Devonport. Both vessels also undertake coastal work.

● A. MacDONALD

MV Warden

TRIALS VESSEL

Ship	Pennant Number	Completion Date	Builder
WARDEN	A368	1989	Richards

Displacement 626 tons **Dimensions** 48m x 10m x 4m **Speed** 15 knots **Complement** 11.

Notes
Built as a Range Maintenance Vessel but now based at Kyle of Lochalsh and operated by the RMAS in support of BUTEC. Note removal of gantry and extended bridge structure.

Spitfire

RESCUE AND TARGET TOWING LAUNCHES (RTTL)

Ship	Pennant Number	Completion Date	Builder
SPITFIRE	4000	1972	James & Stone
HURRICANE	4005	1980	James & Stone
LANCASTER	4006	1981	James & Stone
WELLINGTON	4007	1981	James & Stone

G.R.T. 60 tons **Dimensions** 24m x 5.6m x 1.6m **Speed** 21 knots **Complement** 4/6 They are based at Great Yarmouth and Plymouth.

Notes

The primary tasks for RAF Support craft include target towing, winch training helicopter crews for SAR. The vessels are also used for sea survival training of aircrew.

The Long Range Recovery and Support Craft have been withdrawn from service. SEAL was sold in 2002 and SEAGULL is for sale in 2003. The RTTLs HAMPDEN and HALIFAX were for sale in 2002.

Smit International is contracted to operate SAR and Aircrew Training Vessels on behalf of the MoD. Six new Aircrew Training Vessels were ordered by Smit in January 2002. Three are to be built by FBM Babcock Marine, Rosyth and three in the Philippines. These 27-metre vessels will replace the Spitfire class.

RCTV Arezzo

RAMPED CRAFT LOGISTIC

Vessel	Pennant Number	Completion Date	Builder
ARROMANCHES	L105	1987	James & Stone
ANDALSNES	L107	1984	James & Stone
AKYAB	L109	1984	James & Stone
AACHEN	L110	1986	James & Stone
AREZZO	L111	1986	James & Stone
AUDEMER	L113	1987	James & Stone

Displacement 165 tons **Dimensions** 33m x 8m x 1.5m **Speed** 9 knots
Complement 6.

Notes
Smaller – "all purpose" landing craft capable of carrying up to 96 tons. In service in coastal waters around Cyprus and UK. ARROMANCHES was formerly AGHEILA (re-named 1994 when original vessel was sold). Several vessels sport green and black camouflage scheme.

AIRCRAFT OF THE FLEET AIR ARM

European Helicopter Industries EH101 MERLIN

Variants: HM1
Role: Anti-submarine and Maritime patrol
Engine:3 x Rolls-Royce Turbomeca RTM322 turboshafts developing 2,100 shp
Length: 74' 10" Width: 14' 10" Height: 21' 10" Main rotor diameter: 61'
Max Speed: 167 kts   **Range**: 625 nm
Crew: 3 (Pilot, Observer and Aircrewman)
Avionics: Blue Kestrel 360 degree search radar, Orange Reaper ESM, passive and active sonar systems and AQS903 digital processor.
Armament: 4 lightweight torpedoes or depth charges.
Squadron service: 700 (OEU), 814, 824 Squadrons; 820 to equip in 2003; Flights in the Type 23 frigates LANCASTER and MONMOUTH.
Notes: The Merlin HM1 is an advanced weapon system for the detection and attack of submarines that can also be operated in a number of other roles. Fast and agile for its size, Merlin can be flown by a single pilot and operate off both large and small ships' flight decks in high sea states and severe weather by day and night.
The first front line squadron, 814, was operational in ARK ROYAL by late Spring 2002.

British Aerospace SEA HARRIER

Variants: FA2
Role: Short take off, vertical landing (STOVL) fighter attack and reconnaissance aircraft.
Engine: 1 x 21,500lb thrust Rolls Royce PEGASUS 104, turbofan.
Span 25' 3" **Length** 49' 1" **Height** 12' 0" **Max weight** 26,200lb.
Max speed Mach .9 540 knots **Crew** 1 pilot.
Avionics: Blue Vixen pulse doppler radar
Armament: Up to 4 x AMRAAM Air to Air Missiles. SIDEWINDER air to air missiles. 2 - 30mm Aden cannons with 120 rounds per gun in detachable pods, one either side of the lower fuselage. 1 fuselage centreline and 4 underwing hardpoints. The inner wing stations are capable of carrying 2,000lb of stores and are plumbed for drop tanks. The other positions can carry stores up to 1,000lb in weight. Possible loads include 1,000lb or practice bombs; 190 or 100 gallon drop tanks. A single F95 camera is mounted obliquely in the nose for reconnaissance.
Squadron Service: 800, 801 and 899 squadrons in commission.
Notes: On 1 April 2000, the Royal Navy's Sea Harriers joined the RAF's Harrier GR7s in Joint Force Harrier (JFH), part of 3 Group RAF Strike Command, a maritime air group commanded uniquely by a two-star Admiral based at RAF High Wycombe (other elements of the group include the RAF's Nimrod MR2 maritime reconnaissance fleet and RAF SAR helicopters.) The three Sea Harrier squadrons will continue to be based at Yeovilton but will start to run down in 2004 when 800 Squadron disbands, to be followed by 899 in 2005 and 801 in 2006. They will be replaced by Harrier GR9 aircraft in four squadrons, within JFH, two of which will be "dark blue" manned with the 800 and 801 squadron numbers. The 899 squadron number may also be retained for an operational evaluation unit.

● MoD/CROWN COPYRIGHT

Westland SEA KING

Developed for the Royal Navy from the Sikorsky SH3D, the basic Sea King airframe is used in three different roles. The following details are common to all:
Engines: 2 x 1600shp Rolls Royce Gnome H 1400 – 1 free power turbines.
Rotor Diameter 62' 0" **Length** 54' 9" **Height** 17' 2" **Max Weight** 21,400lb **Max Speed** 125 knots.
The 3 versions are:-

● MoD/CROWN COPYRIGHT

HAR 5 / HAS 6

The HAS6 has improved sonics, deeper dipping active sonar and ESM
Roles: Anti-submarine search and attack. SAR. Transport.
Crew: 2 pilots, 1 observer and 1 aircrewman.
Avionics: Sea Searcher radar; Type 2069 variable depth active/passive sonar AQS 902 passive sonobuoy analyser. Orange Crop passive ESM equipment.
Armament: 4 fuselage hardpoints capable of carrying STINGRAY torpedoes or depth charges. Various flares, markers, grenades and sonobuoys can be carried internally and hand launched. A 7.62mm machine gun can be mounted in the doorway.
Squadron Service: Five HAS6 aircraft are operated by 771 NAS, three for training and two Ships' Flights for Type 22 Frigates. 771 NAS also operates five HAR5 aircraft, primarily in the Search and Rescue (SAR) role.
Notes: The Sea King has been the backbone of the Fleet Air Arm's anti-submarine force for more than 30 years but is now being superseded by the Merlin HM1. The HAR5 continues to provide excellent SAR service in the south west approaches. The HAS6 also has SAR capability, but less complete because of ASW equipment in those aircraft. 819 NAS disbanded in November 2001 at Prestwick, but three aircraft remain, mainly for SAR duties, together with 100 personnel. Some HAS6 airframes, stripped of their radar and sonar, will be used by Commando squadrons while their HC4s are refurbished during 2003.

ASaC 7

Role: Airborne Early Warning. **Crew:** 1 pilot and 2 observers.
Avionics: Upgraded Thales Searchwater radar, Orange Crop passive ESM, Enhanced Communications System, Joint Tactical Information Distribution System (JTIDS)
Squadron Service: 849 HQ, 849A and 849B Flights in commission.
Notes: Used for the airborne surveillance and control of the airspace over a maritime force. Can also be used for surface search utilising their sophisticated, computerised long range radar. During 2003 849A Flight was embarked in ARK ROYAL. 849HQ acts as a training and trials unit at Culdrose. Formerly designated Airborne Early Warning (AEW); now redesignated Airborne Surveillance and Control (ASaC).

● US NAVY

HC 4

Role: Commando assault and utility transport.
Crew: 2 pilots and 1 aircrewman.
Armament: Door mounted 7.62mm machine gun.
Squadron Service: 845, 846 and 848 Squadrons.
Notes: The HC4 has a fixed undercarriage with no sponsons or radome. It is equipped to carry up to 17 troops in the cabin or underslung loads up to 6000 lbs. The three Commando Support squadrons are based at Yeovilton but (together with 847 NAS with its Lynx and Gazelle aircraft) come under the command of the Joint Helicopter Command (JHC) based at Wilton, a tri-Service formation whose purpose is to max-imise the effectiveness of all battlefield helicopters. The Commando Support squadrons train to operate in all environments, from arctic to tropical, and can embark or detach at short notice to support 3 Commando Brigade or as required by the JHC.

• MoD/CROWN COPYRIGHT

Westland LYNX

Variants: HAS 3, HMA 8, AH7.
Roles: Surface search and attack; anti-submarine attack; SAR; troop carrying.
Engines: 2 x 900hp Rolls Royce GEM BS 360-07-26 free shaft turbines.
Rotor diameter: 42' 0" **Length** 39' 1" **Height** 11' 0" **Max Weight** 9,500lb.
Max Speed: 150 knots. **Crew:** 1 pilot and 1 observer.
Avionics: SEA SPRAY radar. Orange Crop passive ESM equipment. Sea Owl Passive Infrared Device (Mk 8).
Armament: External pylons carry up to 4 - SEA SKUA air to surface missiles or 2 x STINGRAY torpedoes, depth charges and markers.
Squadron Service: 702 and 815 squadrons in commission.

Notes: Lynx OEU develops operational tactics for HMA 8 aircraft. 702 is the training squadron. 815 squadron is the parent unit for single aircraft ships flights. Both squadrons are based at Yeovilton. Ships' Flights are divided approximately equally between HAS 3 and HMA 8 aircraft. Another version of the Lynx, the AH7, is operated by 847 NAS in a Commando Support role.

Royal Marine Gazelle AH1 (bottom) and Lynx AH7

Westland GAZELLE AH1

Engine: 1 x 592shp Turbomeca ASTAZOU free power turbine.
Crew: 1 or 2 pilots.

Notes: The Gazelle AH1 is used by 847 NAS based at Yeovilton as a spotter/communications aircraft for the Royal Marines.

OTHER AIRCRAFT TYPES IN ROYAL NAVY SERVICE DURING 2003

● MoD/CROWN COPYRIGHT

British Aerospace HAWK

Engine: 1 x Adour Mk 151 5200 lbs thrust.
Crew: 1 or 2 Pilots (both service and civilian)
Notes: With Fleet Requirements and Aircraft Direction Unit (FRADU) at Culdrose to provide support for training of RN ships, RN Flying Standards Flight and as airborne targets for the Aircraft Direction School.

British Aerospace JETSTREAM T2 and T3

Engines: 2 x 940hp Turbomeca ASTAZOU 16D turboprops. (T3 Garrett turboprops).
Crew: 1 or 2 pilots, 2 student observers plus 3 other seats.
Notes: T2's are used by 750 Squadron at Culdrose for training Fleet Air Arm Observers.T3's are used by the Heron flight at Yeovilton for operational support/communications flying.

Aerospatiale AS365N DAUPHIN 2

Engines: 2 x Turbomeca Arriel 1C1.
Crew: 1 or 2 pilots.
Notes: Operated by British International from Plymouth City Airport under MoD contract. Used to transfer Sea Training staff from shore and between ships operating in the Plymouth sea training areas during work-ups.

GROB G115 D-2

Took over the flying grading and conversion of Rotary to Fixed Wing flying task from the Chipmunk. They are owned and operated by a division of Short Brothers plc and operate from Plymouth City Airport on behalf of 727 NAS (which formed on 6 December 2001).

Royal Navy Historic Flight

The RNHF is supported financially by the Swordfish Heritage Trust. The Historic Flight has been civilianised since 1993.

The current holding of aircraft is:

Flying: 1 Fairey Swordfish, 1 Fairey Firefly.
Under Repair: 2 Fairey Swordfish, 1 Sea Hawk, 1 Sea Fury.

WEAPONS OF THE ROYAL NAVY

Sea Launched Missiles

◀ Trident II D5

The American built Lockheed Martin Trident 2 (D5) submarine launched strategic missiles are Britain's only nuclear weapons and form the UK contribution to the NATO strategic deterrent. 16 missiles, each capable of carrying up to 6 UK manufactured thermonuclear warheads (but currently limited to 4 under current government policy), are aboard each of the Vanguard class SSBNs. Trident has a maximum range of 12,000 km and is powered by a three stage rocket motor. Launch weight is 60 tonnes, overall length and width are 13.4 metres and 2.1 metres respectively.

Sea Wolf

Short range rapid reaction anti-missile and anti-aircraft weapon. The complete weapon system, including radars and fire control computers, is entirely automatic in operation. Type 22 frigates carry two sextuple Sea Wolf launchers but the subsequent Type 23 frigates carry 32 Vertical Launch Seawolf (VLS) in a silo on the foredeck. Basic missile data: weight 82 kg, length 1.9 m, wingspan 56 cm, range c.56 km, warhead 13.4 kg. The VLS missile is basically similar but has jettisonable tandem boost rocket motors.

Harpoon

The Boeing (McDonnell Douglas) Harpoon is a sophisticated anti-ship missile using a combination of inertial guidance and active radar homing to attack targets out to a range of 130 km, cruising at Mach 0.9 and carrying a 227 kg warhead. Currently fitted to the Batch II Type 22 and Type 23 frigates. It is powered by a lightweight turbojet but is accelerated at launch by a booster rocket. The Royal Navy also deploys the UGM-84 submarine launched version aboard its Swiftsure and Trafalgar class SSNs.

Sea Dart

A medium range area defence anti aircraft missile powered by a ramjet and solid fuel booster rocket. Maximum effective range is in the order of 80 km and the missile accelerates to a speed of Mach 3.5. It forms the main armament of the Type 42 destroyers. Missile weight 550 kg, length 4.4 m, wingspan 0.91 m.

Tomahawk (BGM-109)

This is a land attack cruise missile with a range of 1600 km and can be launched from a variety of platforms including surface ships and submarines. Some 65 of the latter version were purchased from America to arm Trafalgar class SSNs with the first being delivered to the Royal Navy for trials during 1998. Tomahawk is fired in a disposal container from the submarine's conventional torpedo tubes and is then accelerated to its subsonic cruising speed by a booster rocket motor before a lightweight F-107 turbojet takes over for the cruise. Its extremely accurate guidance system means that small targets can be hit with precision at maximum range, as was dramatically illustrated in the Gulf War and Afghanistan. Total weight of the submarine version, including its launch capsule is 1816 kg, it carries a 450 kg warhead, length is 6.4 metres and wingspan (fully extended) 2.54 m. Fitted in some S and T class submarines.

Air Launched Missiles

Sea Skua

A small anti ship missile developed by British Aerospace arming the Lynx helicopters carried by various frigates and destroyers. The missile weighs 147 kg, has a length of 2.85 m and a span of 62 cm. Powered by solid fuel booster and sustainer rocket motors, it has a range of over 15 km at high subsonic speed. Sea Skua is particularly effective against patrol vessels and fast attack craft, as was demonstrated in both the Falklands and Gulf Wars.

Sidewinder

This is one of the world's most successful short range air to air missiles. The latest AIM-9L version carried by Sea Harriers uses a heat seeking infra red guidance system and has a range of 18 km. Powered by a solid fuel rocket motor boosting it to speeds of Mach 2.5, it weighs 86.6 kg and is 2.87 m long.

AMRAAM

The Hughes AIM-120 Advanced Medium Range Air To Air Missile arms the latest Sea Harrier FA.2 and has a range of around 50 km. Weight 157 kg, length 3.65 m. Coupled with the Blue Vixen multi mode radar, the AMRAAM gives a substantial boost to the aircraft's capability as an air defence interceptor, allowing Beyond Visual Range (BVR) engagements.

Guns

114mm Vickers Mk8

The Royal Navy's standard medium calibre general purpose gun which arms the later Type 22s, Type 23 frigates and Type 42 destroyers. Rate of fire: 25 rounds/min. Range: 22,000 m. Weight of Shell: 21 kg.

Goalkeeper

A highly effective automatic Close in Weapons System (CIWS) designed to shoot down missiles and aircraft which have evaded the outer layers of a ships defences. The complete system, designed and built in Holland, is on an autonomous mounting and includes radars, fire control computers and a 7-barrel 30 mm Gatling gun firing 4200 rounds/min. Goalkeeper is designed to engage targets between 350 and 1500 metres away.

Phalanx

A US built CIWS designed around the Vulcan 20 mm rotary cannon. Rate of fire is 3000 rounds/min and effective range is c.1500 m. Fitted in Type 42, HM Ships OCEAN and FEARLESS.

GCM-AO3 30mm

This mounting carries two Oerlikon 30 mm guns each capable of firing 650 rounds/min. Effective range is 3000 m. Fitted to Type 22 frigates and the LPDs.

DS30B 30mm

Single 30 mm mounting carrying an Oerlikon 30 mm gun. Fitted to Type 23 frigates and various patrol vessels and MCMVs.

GAM BO 20mm

A simple hand operated mounting carrying a single Oerlikon KAA 200 automatic cannon firing 1000 rounds/min. maximum range is 2000 m. Carried by most of the fleet's major warships except the Type 23 frigates.

20mm Mk.7A

The design of this simple but reliable weapon dates back to World War II but it still provides a useful increase in firepower, particularly for auxiliary vessels and RFAs. Rate of fire 500-800 rounds/min.

Torpedoes

Stingray

A lightweight anti submarine torpedo which can be launched from ships, helicopters or aircraft. In effect it is an undersea guided missile with a range of 11 km at 45 knots or 7.5 km at 60 knots. Length 2.1 m, diameter 330 mm. Aboard Type 42s and Type 22s Stingray is fired from triple tubes forming part of the Ships Torpedo Weapon System (STWS) but the newer Type 23s have the Magazine Torpedo Launch System (MTLS) with internal launch tubes.

Mk24 Tigerfish

A wire guided heavyweight torpedo carried by all Royal Navy submarines. Mainly designed for the anti-submarine role but its 134 kg warhead is equally effective against surface vessels. Propulsion is by means of a powerful two speed electric motor giving a range of 29 km at 24 knots or 13 km at 35 knots. Diameter is the standard 533 mm, and overall length approximately 6.5 m.

Spearfish

A complex heavyweight torpedo now entering service after a protracted and extensive development period. Claimed by the manufacturers to be the world's fastest torpedo, capable of over 70 kts, its sophisticated guidance system includes an onboard acoustic processing suite and tactical computer backed up by a command and control wire link to the parent submarine. Spearfish is fired from the standard submarine torpedo tube, but it is slightly shorter than Tigerfish and utilises an advanced turbine engine for higher performance.

At the end of the line ...

Readers may well find other warships afloat which are not mentioned in this book. The majority have fulfilled a long and useful life and are now relegated to non-seagoing duties. The following list gives details of their current duties:

Pennant No	Ship	Remarks
	BRITANNIA	Ex Royal Yacht at Leith. Open to the public.
	CAROLINE	RNR Drill Ship at Belfast, Northern Ireland.
A134	RAME HEAD	Escort Maintenance Vessel – Royal Marines Training Ship in Fareham Creek (Portsmouth)
C35	BELFAST	World War II Cruiser Museum ship – Pool of London. Open to the public daily . Tel: 020 7940 6300
D23	BRISTOL	Type 82 Destroyer – Sea Cadet Training Ship at Portsmouth.
D73 S17	CAVALIER OCELOT	World War II Destroyer & Oberon class Submarine Museum Ships at Chatham. Partially open to the public. Tel: 01634 823800
F126 S21 M1115	PLYMOUTH ONYX BRONINGTON	Type 12 Frigate, Oberon class Submarine & Ton class Minesweeper. Museum Ships at Birkenhead, Wirral. Open to the public daily. Tel: 0151 650 1573
S67	ALLIANCE	Submarine – Museum Ship at Gosport Open to the public daily. Tel: 023 92 511349
M1151 M1154	IVESTON KELLINGTON	(Thurrock) } Static Sea Cadet (Stockton upon Tees) } Training Vessels

At the time of publishing (December 2002) the following ships were laid up in long term storage or awaiting sale.

PORTSMOUTH: Intrepid; Fearless; Boxer; Brave; Coventry; London; Scylla.

PLYMOUTH: Courageous; Conqueror; Valiant; Warspite.

ROSYTH: Resolution; Renown; Repulse; Revenge; Swiftsure; Dreadnought; Churchill.